Greetings, goats!

MARVELS ANIMALS 50

GOATS

KATE RIGGS

CREATIVE EDUCATION | CREATIVE PAPERBACKS

YOU'VE GOAT TO BE KIDDING ME.

table of contents

Greetings, Goats! 1
Goats on Pastures 7
Colorful Hair 8
Hooves and Horns 10
Time to Eat! 12
Kidding Around 14
What Do Goats Do? 16
Farewell, Goats! 18
Picture a Goat 20
Words to Know 22
Read More 22
Websites 22
Index 24

Published by Creative Education and Creative Paperbacks
P.O. Box 227, Mankato, Minnesota 56002
Creative Education and Creative Paperbacks
are imprints of The Creative Company
www.thecreativecompany.us

Design by Wyeth Morgan
Art direction by Blue Design (www.bluedes.com)

Images by flickr/Biodiversity Heritage Library, cover (left); Getty Images/Antagain, 10–11, Brian Nimens, 3, 20–21, imageBROKER/Justus de Cuveland, 18–19, saulgranda, 24; Pexels/Jacek Plak, 17, Max S., 1, Ralph, 8–9, Soundarapandian MS, 14–15, Thanh Luu, 2; Unsplash/Alejandro Luengo, cover (right), Amandeep Chaudhary, 23, Milana Jovanov, 13, Onur Tuna, 6–7, Raisa Milova, cover (middle), Timur Garifov, 4; Wikimedia Commons/Dagurba, 16

Library of Congress Cataloging-in-Publication Data
Names: Riggs, Kate, author.
Title: Goats / Kate Riggs.
Other titles: Goats (Marvels)
Description: Mankato, Minnesota : Creative Education / Creative Paperbacks, [2026] | Series: Marvels | Includes bibliographical references and index. | Audience: Ages 4-7 | Audience: Grades K-1 | Summary: "An introduction to goats, this beginning reader features eye-catching photographs, humorous captions, and basic life science facts about these horned roamers. Includes a labeled image guide, glossary, and further resources"– Provided by publisher.
Identifiers: LCCN 2024044717 (print) | LCCN 2024044718 (ebook) | ISBN 9798889895749 (library binding) | ISBN 9781682777077 (paperback) | ISBN 9798889895800 (ebook)
Subjects: LCSH: Goats–Juvenile literature.
Classification: LCC SF383.35 .R546 2026 (print) | LCC SF383.35 (ebook) | DDC 636.3/–dc23/eng/20241223
LC record available at https://lccn.loc.gov/2024044717
LC ebook record available at https://lccn.loc.gov/2024044718

Printed in India

Some goats are farm animals. Other goats are wild. Groups of goats are kept on **pastures**.

NICE SPOTS, MAN.
NICE STRIPES, BUDDY.

Hairy goats are many colors. They have white, brown, gray, or black hair. Some goats have hair with spots or stripes of color.

Goat tails are short and point up. Goat hooves have two toes. Most goats have two horns.

WHY DO I
ONLY HAVE TWO?

Goats eat many things. They eat grasses and weeds. They eat woody plants and leaves.

TASTY
FLOWER!

Baby goats are called kids. They drink milk at first. Then they start eating plants.

GOAT KIDS CAN STAND JUST MINUTES AFTER BIRTH.

Curious goats climb everything. They try to get out of their pen or fence.

BAH,
BAH!

Farewell, goats!

[Picture a Goat]

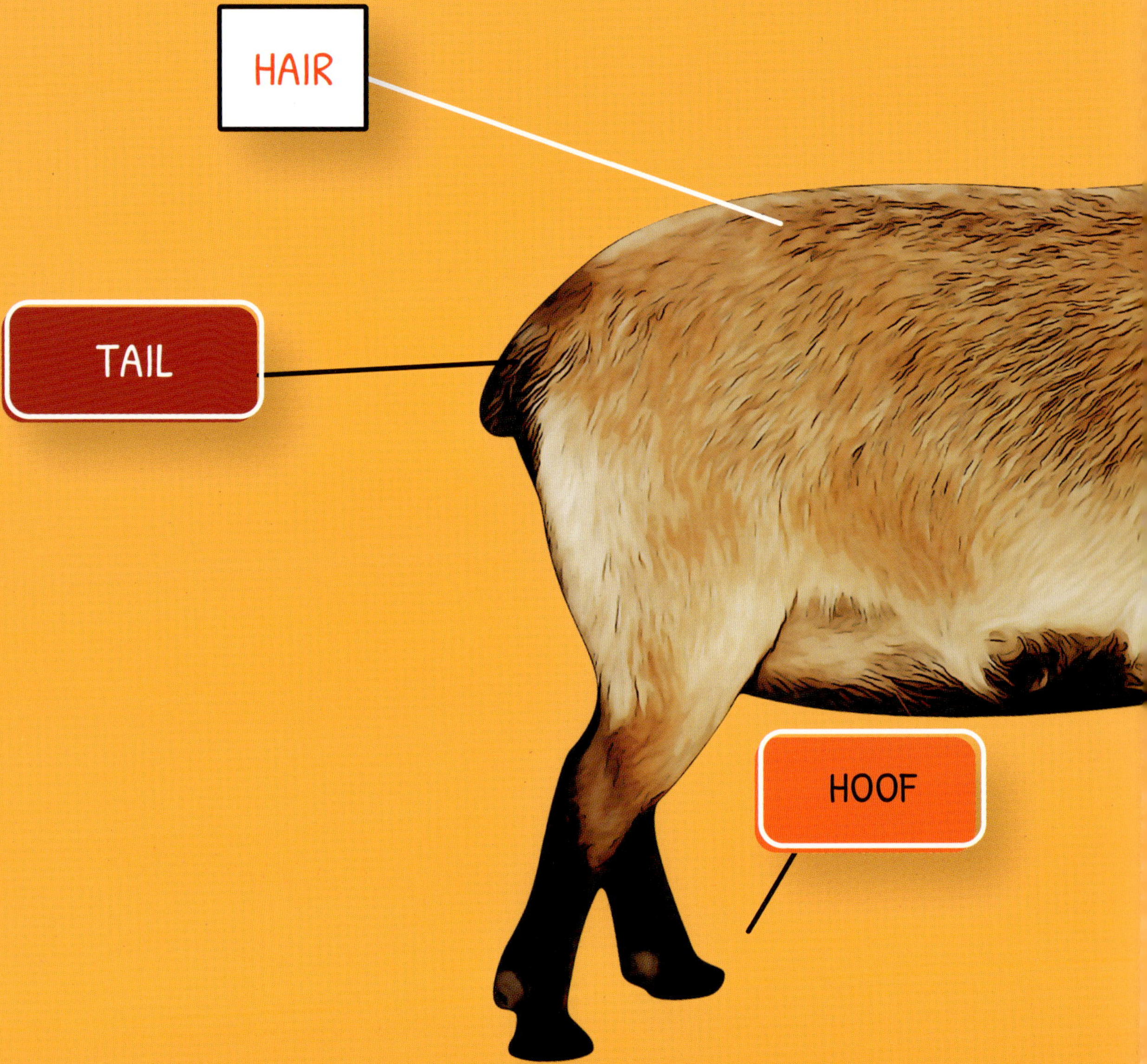

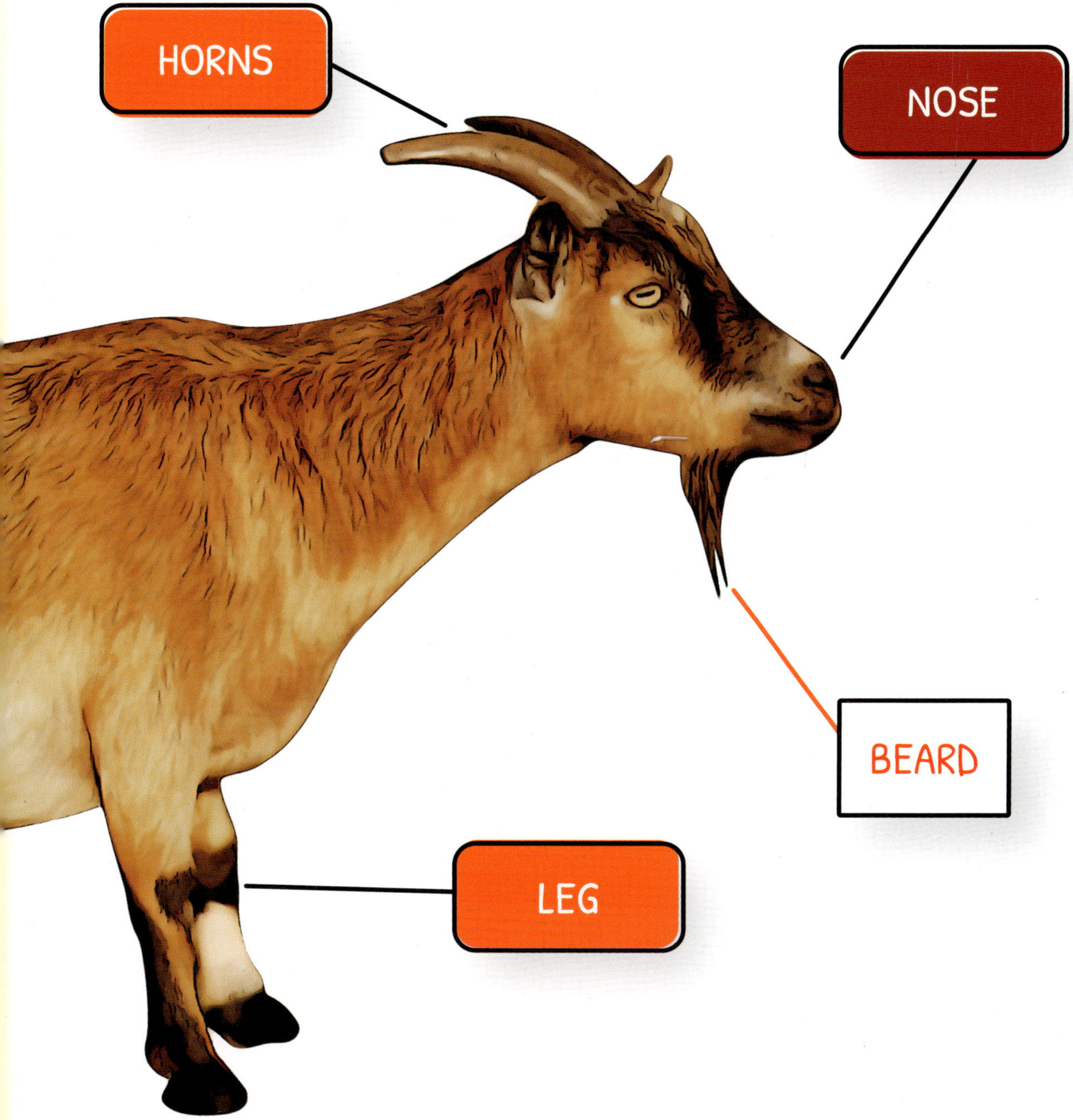
HORNS
NOSE
BEARD
LEG

WORDS TO KNOW

curious: wanting to know more about something

hoof: the horny part of a goat's foot

pasture: land covered with grass and other plants

READ MORE

Anderhagen, Anna. *Goat Kids: A First Look.* Minneapolis: Lerner Publications, 2025.

Sabelko, Rebecca. *Goats.* Minneapolis: Bellwether Media, 2024.

WEBSITES

Britannica Kids: Goat
https://kids.britannica.com/students/article/goat/274580

Read more about domestic and wild goats.

SPCA Kids: Goats
https://kids.spcaeducation.org.nz/animal-care/goats/

Learn about how to raise and care for goats.

INDEX

climbing, 16

colors, 9

farms, 7

food, 12, 15

hair, 9, 20

hooves, 10, 20

horns, 10, 21

kids, 15

pastures, 7

tails, 10, 20